SEA OTTER

Amazing Facts About Ocean's Cleverest Mammals for Kids

Dylanna Press

Copyright © 2026 by Dylanna Press
Author: Tyler Grady

All rights reserved. No part of this publication may be reproduced, stored in a retrieval system, or transmitted by any means, including electronic, mechanical, photocopying, or otherwise, without prior written permission of the publisher.

Although the publisher has taken all reasonable care in the preparation of this book, we make no warranty about the accuracy or completeness of its content and, to the maximum extent permitted, disclaim all liability arising from its use.

Trademarks: Dylanna Press is a registered trademark of Dylanna Publishing, Inc. and may not be used without written permission.

ISBN: 978-1-64790-482-1
Publisher: Dylanna Publishing, Inc.
First Edition: 2026

10 9 8 7 6 5 4 3 2 1

For information about special discounts for bulk purchases, please contact:

Dylanna Publishing, Inc.
www.dylannapublishing.com

Contents

Meet the Sea Otter   7

What Do Sea Otters Look Like?   8

Where Do Sea Otters Live?   11

Master of the Kelp Forest: Sea Otter Adaptations   12

What Do Sea Otters Eat?   15

Life in the Raft   16

On the Move   18

A Day in the Life   20

Mating and Birth   23

Growing Up Sea Otter   24

Sea Otters and Their Ecosystem   27

Natural Predators   28

Challenges and Threats   31

Life Span and Population   32

Conclusion   35

Test Your Sea Otter Knowledge!   36

STEM Challenge: Think Like a Scientist!   37

Word Search   38

Glossary   39

Resources and References   40

Index   41

Fun Fact: Sea otters do almost everything while floating on their backs—even sleeping!

Meet the Sea Otter

SPLASH! A furry head pops up from the waves. Floating on its back like a tiny boat, a sea otter clutches a sea urchin in its paws. With a rock balanced on its chest, it starts hammering away at its spiny breakfast. Welcome to the world of one of the ocean's most charming residents!

Sea otters are marine mammals that live along the rocky coasts of the North Pacific Ocean. From the icy waters of Alaska and Russia down to the shores of California, these playful animals spend almost their entire lives at sea. Unlike river otters that split their time between land and water, sea otters do nearly everything while floating—eating, resting, grooming, and even caring for their young.

The sea otter (*Enhydra lutris*) belongs to the weasel family, making it the largest member of that group—but it's also the smallest marine mammal in the ocean. What sea otters lack in size, they make up for in intelligence, curiosity, and skill.

There are three main types of sea otters living in different regions. Russian sea otters are found in Asian waters, northern sea otters live along the coasts of Alaska and Canada, and southern sea otters—also called California sea otters—inhabit the central California coast. Each group has adapted to its environment, but all share the same clever behaviors and playful nature.

Sea otters are famous for using tools. They're one of the few animals that carry rocks to crack open shellfish, turning their chest into a floating dinner table. They also hold paws or wrap themselves in kelp while resting, helping them stay together and avoid drifting away.

Once hunted nearly to extinction for their incredibly soft fur, sea otters have made a remarkable recovery thanks to conservation efforts. Today, they play a vital role in keeping coastal ecosystems healthy—especially kelp forests—making them not just adorable ocean mammals, but true heroes of the sea.

What Do Sea Otters Look Like?

Sea otters have one of the most recognizable appearances in the animal kingdom. With their round faces, bright eyes, and long whiskers, they often look curious and alert. When floating on their backs with their paws folded on their chest, they can even resemble tiny, furry swimmers relaxing at the surface.

Male sea otters are larger than females. Adult males usually grow 4 to 5 feet (1.2 to 1.5 meters) long and weigh between 70 and 100 pounds (32 to 45 kilograms). Females are smaller, measuring about 3 to 4 feet (0.9 to 1.2 meters) and weighing 50 to 70 pounds (23 to 32 kilograms). Despite the size difference, both sexes share the same compact, streamlined body shape.

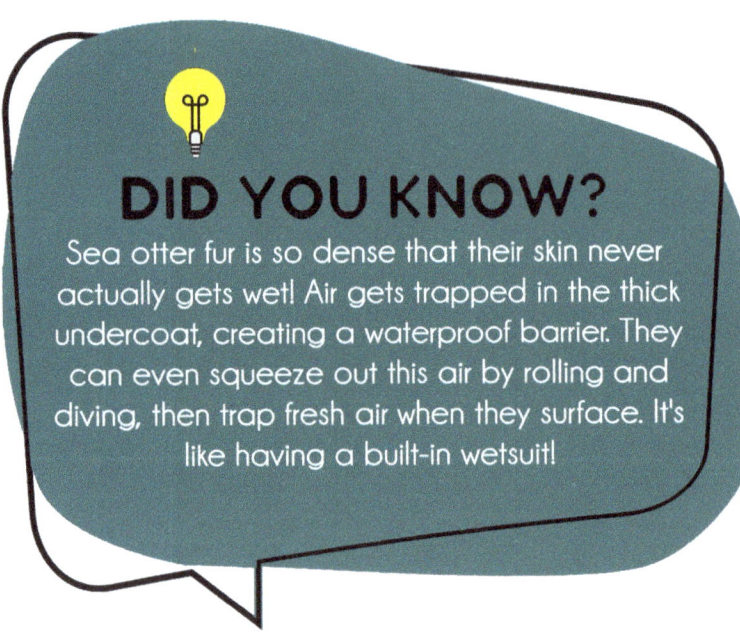

DID YOU KNOW?
Sea otter fur is so dense that their skin never actually gets wet! Air gets trapped in the thick undercoat, creating a waterproof barrier. They can even squeeze out this air by rolling and diving, then trap fresh air when they surface. It's like having a built-in wetsuit!

A sea otter's most remarkable feature is its fur—the densest of any animal on Earth. With up to one million hairs per square inch, this thick coat traps air next to the skin and keeps the otter warm in icy water. Their fur ranges in color from deep brown to lighter chestnut, often with silver-tipped hairs that give older otters a frosted appearance.

Sea otter faces are full of detail. Small, dark eyes help them stay alert to danger, while a short black nose and sensitive whiskers (called vibrissae) help them locate food underwater. Their small ears can close tightly when diving, keeping water out.

Their bodies are built for swimming. Sea otters have short, flattened tails that act like rudders, helping them steer through the water. Their front paws are small, flexible, and highly dexterous, allowing them to groom their fur, hold food, and use tools with surprising precision. In contrast, their back feet are large, flat, and webbed, working like flippers to power them through the ocean.

Fun Fact: Most sea otters live within about a mile of the shore and prefer shallow coastal waters.

Where Do Sea Otters Live?

Sea otters live along the cold, nutrient-rich coastlines of the North Pacific Ocean. They are found in coastal waters from Russia and Alaska down to central California. These marine mammals depend on nearshore habitats where food is plentiful and kelp forests grow thick and tall.

Most sea otters stay close to shore. They usually live within about a mile of land and prefer shallow waters less than 130 feet (40 meters) deep. Rocky sea floors, kelp forests, and sheltered coves provide the perfect combination of food, protection, and resting places.

Alaska is home to the largest sea otter population in the world. About 90 percent of all sea otters live in Alaskan waters, especially around the Aleutian Islands, Prince William Sound, and the islands of Southeast Alaska. These cold waters are rich in shellfish and other prey, allowing sea otters to thrive.

In California, southern sea otters live along roughly 300 miles of coastline from Half Moon Bay to Point Conception. Monterey Bay sits at the center of their range and contains some of the most important kelp forests for this population. Because this group is smaller and more isolated, it is especially vulnerable to threats like oil spills and disease.

A smaller population of sea otters lives along the coast of British Columbia, Canada. These otters were reintroduced from Alaska in the 1960s and 1970s and have successfully established themselves along the rugged shores of Vancouver Island.

Rather than defending strict territories, sea otters use home ranges—areas where they regularly feed and rest. Males often roam across larger stretches of coastline, while females with pups stay in smaller, safer areas with reliable food sources.

Kelp forests are essential to sea otter survival. These underwater habitats provide food, shelter from storms, and safe places to rest. Sea otters often wrap themselves in kelp while floating to keep from drifting away—using the forest like a natural anchor.

Master of the Kelp Forest: Sea Otter Adaptations

Sea otters are perfectly designed for life in the cold Pacific Ocean. Every part of their body helps them survive in a challenging marine environment.

- **The Ultimate Fur Coat:** Sea otters have the densest fur in the animal kingdom—up to 1 million hairs per square inch! This incredible coat has two layers. Dense underfur traps air to keep them warm, while longer guard hairs repel water. The system works so well that their skin rarely gets wet, even in freezing seas.

- **Built-In Life Jacket:** Unlike seals and whales that rely on blubber to stay warm, sea otters depend entirely on their fur and fast metabolism. Their bones are less dense than those of most marine animals, which helps them float easily. That's why sea otters can bob on the surface so effortlessly!

- **Tool-Using Hands:** Sea otters have highly skilled front paws with semi-retractable claws. They are one of the few marine mammals that regularly use tools. Many carry a favorite rock in a loose pocket of skin under their arm and use it like a hammer to crack open hard shells.

- **Powerful Swimming Equipment:** Large, webbed hind feet work like swim fins, pushing sea otters through the water. They can swim up to 5.6 miles per hour (9 km/h) and dive as deep as 330 feet (100 meters)—though they usually stay in much shallower water.

- **Sensitive Whiskers**: Long, stiff whiskers help sea otters find food in murky water. These whiskers can detect tiny movements and vibrations, allowing them to locate hidden shellfish even when they can't see clearly.

- **Oxygen Storage System:** Sea otters can hold their breath for up to 5 minutes while diving. Their blood contains extra red blood cells that store oxygen, helping them stay underwater longer during hunts.

- **Heat Production Machine:** To stay warm in cold water, sea otters have incredibly fast metabolisms—about 2.5 times faster than other mammals their size. They must eat 20–25% of their body weight every day just to fuel this internal heating system. That's like a 60-pound kid eating 15 pounds of food daily!

Together, these adaptations help sea otters survive in cold ocean waters and thrive in kelp forest habitats.

Fun Fact: Sea otters spend up to 40% of their day grooming their fur to keep it clean and waterproof.

SEA OTTER MATH

" A sea otter eats about 25% of its body weight every day.

If a sea otter weighs 80 pounds, how much food does it need each day? "

A: 20 POUNDS

What Do Sea Otters Eat?

Sea otters are skilled carnivores with a taste for seafood, and their diet reflects their role as one of the ocean's top predators in coastal ecosystems.

Young sea otters begin by eating small, soft-bodied animals like shrimp and small crabs. As they grow, they learn to handle harder prey and even start using tools to crack open tough shells.

Adult sea otters have strong jaws and flat molars, perfect for crunching clams, mussels, sea urchins, crabs, and snails. Many otters develop favorite foods and hunting styles, sometimes specializing in certain prey or foraging areas.

Sea otters need to eat a lot—up to 25% of their body weight daily—to fuel their high metabolism and stay warm in cold water. That's like a 100-pound person eating 25 pounds of food every day!

They dive to the seafloor, using sensitive whiskers to locate prey hidden in sand or rocks. Otters bring their catch to the surface and eat while floating on their backs, often using their chest like a dinner table.

Fun Fact: Their powerful jaws can crush shells that would break human teeth!

They're one of the few non-human animals known to use tools—typically rocks—to smash open hard shells. Some even carry favorite rocks in loose skin folds under their forearms.

By eating sea urchins, sea otters help protect kelp forests, which support a wide variety of marine life. Their feeding habits make them not just impressive hunters, but also key players in keeping ocean ecosystems healthy.

Life in the Raft

One of the most charming sights in nature is a group of sea otters floating together on their backs, sometimes holding paws as they rest on the water. These groups, called rafts, are an important part of sea otter social life.

Rafts can vary widely in size. Some include just a few otters, while others—especially in Alaska—can contain hundreds of animals drifting together. Along the California coast, rafts are usually smaller, often made up of 10 to 100 otters.

Rafts are often organized by gender. Female rafts usually include mothers with pups and other adult females. Male rafts are made up of bachelor males and older individuals. During breeding season, these groups mix as males and females come together to mate.

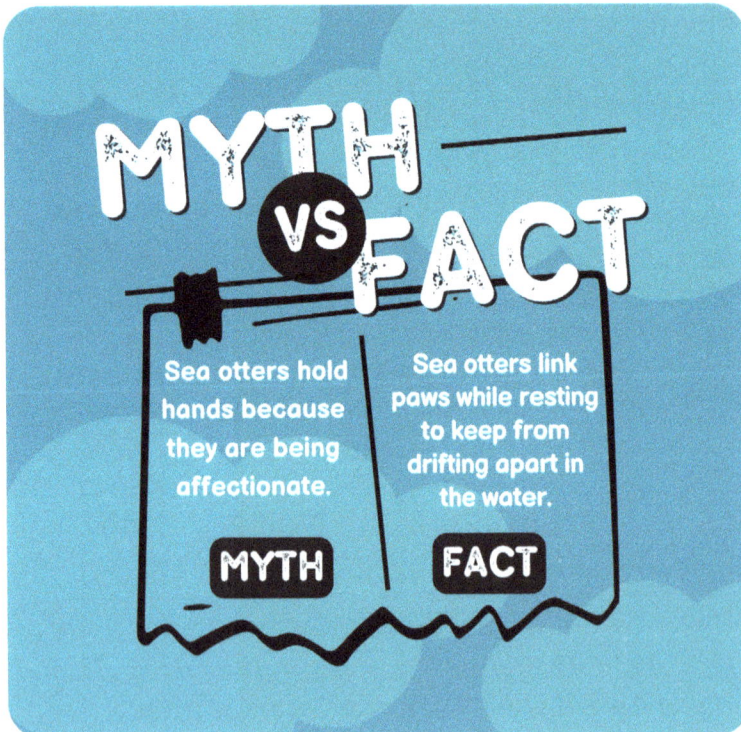

The famous paw-holding behavior isn't just adorable—it's practical. By linking paws while resting, sea otters help keep from drifting apart. They may also wrap strands of kelp around their bodies like natural anchors, helping them stay in place.

Sea otters are social animals. Within rafts, they groom themselves and sometimes one another, rest close together, and stay alert to what's happening around them. Young otters learn important survival skills by watching the adults nearby.

Communication is an important part of raft life. Mothers and pups use distinctive squeaks and whimpers to find each other. Adults make different sounds to signal alarm, contentment, or aggression. During mating season, males produce loud calls that can carry across the water.

Living in a group also improves safety. A large raft can spot danger more quickly than a single otter, providing early warning—especially for vulnerable pups.

Rafts change throughout the day as otters leave to hunt and return to rest. Still, many sea otters gather in the same areas and float with familiar companions day after day, forming loose but lasting social bonds.

Fun Fact: Sea otters can drift several miles while resting—sometimes waking up in a completely different spot than where they fell asleep!

On the Move

Unlike whales that migrate thousands of miles each year, sea otters usually stay close to home. They prefer familiar coastal waters and rarely travel long distances unless food becomes scarce or conditions change.

Each sea otter uses a home range along the coast, often covering about 2 to 5 miles (3 to 8 kilometers) of shoreline. Males generally roam over larger areas than females, especially during breeding season. These home ranges often overlap, and otters usually avoid conflict by spacing themselves out naturally.

Daily movement is closely tied to feeding and tides. Sea otters are most active during daylight hours, making many short foraging dives throughout the day. They often rest during high tide, when prey can be harder to reach, and become more active again when tides drop.

Seasonal movements are usually limited. Some sea otters shift slightly to find better food sources or calmer water during winter storms, but if conditions are good, many remain in the same general area year-round.

Young males are the most likely to travel farther. As they search for their own home ranges, some have been recorded moving more than 100 miles (160 kilometers) from where they were born. Even so, most sea otters settle much closer to home.

Despite their relaxed appearance, sea otters are capable swimmers. They typically cruise at 3 to 5 miles per hour (5 to 8 km/h) and can reach speeds of nearly 6 miles per hour (9 km/h) when needed. Their large, webbed hind feet provide strong propulsion, while their front paws help steer.

Sea otters often float on their backs to rest and groom, but when traveling purposefully, they usually swim belly-down. This helps them move efficiently while protecting their carefully maintained fur.

A Day in the Life

A sea otter's day revolves around three main activities: eating, grooming, and resting—and each one is essential for survival.

At dawn, sea otters often float together in their rafts as they slowly wake up. The first task of the day is grooming. This isn't just for looks—it's a matter of survival. Sea otters spend 2–3 hours each day grooming their fur to keep it clean, fluffy, and waterproof.

The grooming process is thorough. Using their front paws, sea otters work air into their dense undercoat, clean their whiskers, and carefully maintain every inch of fur. They can even reach their own backs by rolling and twisting in the water like furry acrobats.

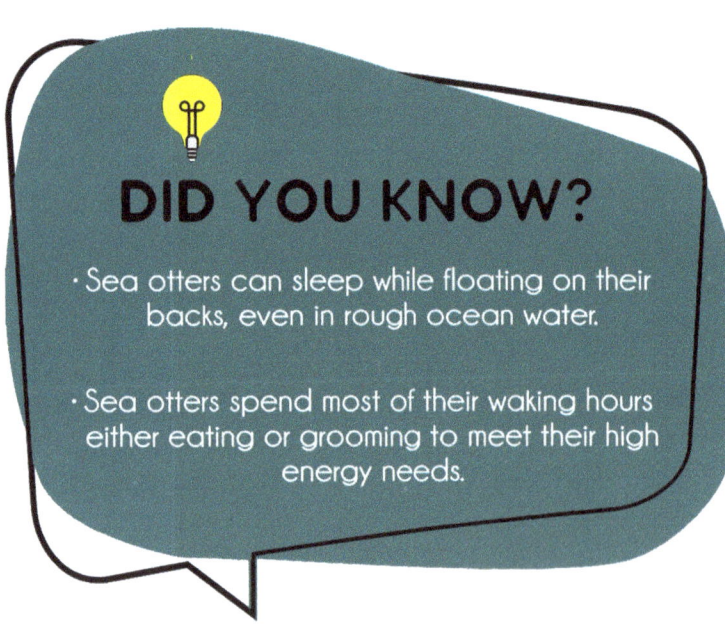

DID YOU KNOW?

- Sea otters can sleep while floating on their backs, even in rough ocean water.
- Sea otters spend most of their waking hours either eating or grooming to meet their high energy needs.

After grooming comes breakfast—the first of many meals. Sea otters make 10–15 dives during a foraging session, usually staying underwater for 1–3 minutes at a time. They gather shellfish, crabs, and sea urchins, then return to the surface to eat while floating on their backs.

Midday is often a time for rest, especially on calm, sunny days. Sea otters float together in rafts, sometimes holding paws or wrapping themselves in kelp. Some even nap with their paws over their eyes to block the bright sun.

In the afternoon, sea otters forage again and spend more time grooming. During breeding season, there is increased social activity, while mothers devote extra time to caring for and teaching their pups important survival skills.

As evening approaches, sea otters often gather in larger rafts for warmth and safety. Anchored by kelp and surrounded by companions, they bob gently on the ocean swells, ready to repeat the same essential routine the next day.

Although the pattern stays mostly the same, daily life can change with the weather and food supply. Stormy days mean resting in sheltered waters, while rich feeding areas may lead to longer meals. No matter the conditions, sea otter life follows a simple rhythm: eat, groom, rest—repeat.

Fun Fact: They have favorite rocks that they keep and reuse—like having a favorite fork!

Mating and Birth

Sea otter breeding can happen throughout the year, though most mating occurs in spring and early summer. During this time, mature males establish breeding areas along the coast and use loud vocal calls to attract females.

Male sea otters usually reach maturity at 5–7 years old, while females mature earlier, around 3–4 years. During breeding season, males become more aggressive toward other males as they compete for access to females, especially in areas with good feeding opportunities.

After mating, males and females separate. Female sea otters raise their pups alone, providing all care without help from the male.

Pregnancy lasts about 4–5 months, though it can be longer because of delayed implantation. This adaptation allows females to time the birth of their pups for periods when food is plentiful and conditions are safest.

Female sea otters usually give birth to a single pup while floating on their backs in the water. Twins are extremely rare. Newborn pups weigh about 3–5 pounds (1.5–2.3 kg) and are born with extra-fluffy fur that keeps them floating like little corks.

From the moment it is born, the pup depends entirely on its mother. She carries the pup on her chest, grooms it constantly, and teaches it essential survival skills. Mothers and pups communicate with soft squeaks and whimpers to stay connected.

Pups nurse for about 4–6 months, though they begin tasting solid food earlier by grabbing pieces of their mother's catch. The mother's milk is rich in fat, helping pups grow quickly and develop their thick adult fur.

NEWBORN PUP STATS
- Birth weight: 3–5 lb (1.5–2.3 kg)
- Swimming: Immediately (but not diving)
- Diving: Around 2 months
- Weaning: 4–6 months

Timing is critical for survival. Pups born in spring or summer have the best chance of success, giving them months to learn how to swim, dive, and hunt before winter arrives. Choosing calm, food-rich waters can make the difference between life and death.

Growing Up Sea Otter

Raising a sea otter pup is one of nature's most demanding parenting jobs. For months, mother sea otters devote nearly every moment to caring for their young. It is exhausting, challenging, and essential for a pup's survival.

Newborn pups are helpless, yet perfectly adapted for their floating nursery. Their natal fur is so fluffy and dense that they cannot sink. Instead, they bob on the surface like little corks. This is critical, since pups cannot swim or dive for their first two months.

Mothers act as living rafts, carrying their pups on their chests while floating on their backs. When a mother dives to search for food, she leaves her pup floating safely on the surface. The pup's dense fur keeps it afloat until she returns.

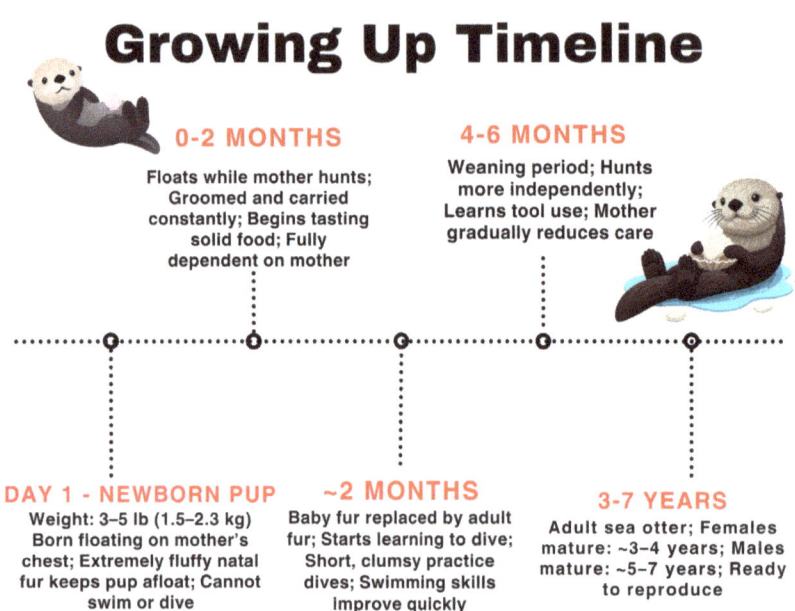

Learning begins right away. Pups closely watch their mothers and learn by observation. Mothers groom their pups often, helping keep their fur clean and waterproof. They also bring back different prey, allowing pups to investigate and begin tasting solid food.

At around two months of age, a pup's adult fur replaces its baby fluff, making diving possible. Early dives are short and awkward, but pups improve quickly with practice.

Mothers teach their pups everything they need to survive: which foods to eat, how to use rocks to crack shells, where to find safe resting places, and how to behave around other otters. Some pups even learn tool-use techniques passed down through generations.

Weaning usually occurs between 4 and 6 months. The timing depends on the pup's skill level and the mother's condition. When food is scarce, mothers may continue caring for their pups longer.

Independence often comes suddenly. Once a mother decides her pup is ready, she leaves. From that moment on, the young sea otter must rely on everything it has learned to survive on its own.

Fun Fact: A single sea otter can eat hundreds of sea urchins each year—helping entire kelp forests grow back and thrive!

Sea Otters and Their Ecosystem

Sea otters aren't just adorable ocean mammals—they play a powerful role in shaping coastal ecosystems. Every dive, bite, and floating meal affects the plants and animals around them.

Urchin Controllers: Sea otters help control sea urchin populations. Sea urchins eat kelp, and without otters, their numbers can grow quickly. Too many urchins can destroy kelp forests, turning them into underwater "urchin barrens."

Kelp Forest Protectors: By eating sea urchins, sea otters protect kelp forests. These towering underwater plants provide food and shelter for hundreds of species, from fish and crabs to seabirds and marine mammals.

Food Web Stabilizers: Sea otters influence many levels of the food chain. Healthy kelp forests support more fish, which attract larger predators. This chain reaction, called a **trophic cascade**, helps keep ocean ecosystems balanced.

Invertebrate Managers: In addition to sea urchins, sea otters hunt crabs, clams, mussels, and sea stars. By feeding on many different prey species, they prevent any one population from growing out of control.

Nutrient Recyclers: Even sea otter waste helps the ecosystem. Their droppings release nutrients back into the water, supporting tiny organisms that form the base of the marine food web.

Coastal Guardians: Kelp forests protected by sea otters help reduce wave energy, protecting coastlines from erosion. These calmer waters create safer habitats for marine life and benefit humans as well.

Ocean Health Indicators: Because sea otters live near the top of the food chain and remain in coastal waters, scientists study them to understand ocean health. When otter populations struggle, it can signal problems in the marine environment.

Protecting sea otters means protecting entire coastal ecosystems. These playful animals help keep the ocean healthy, balanced, and full of life.

DID YOU KNOW?

Sea otters are considered keystone species—animals whose impact on their ecosystem is much larger than their numbers. Without them, entire underwater habitats can collapse!

Natural Predators

Life as a coastal marine mammal means sea otters must stay constantly alert. Although they are smart, agile, and social, sea otters are relatively small and face threats from some of the ocean's most powerful predators.

Great White Sharks: Along the California coast, great white sharks are the most common cause of sea otter deaths. Sharks do not hunt otters intentionally. Instead, they mistake floating otters for seals. After a test bite, sharks usually release the otter—but the injury is often fatal.

Killer Whales (Orcas): In Alaska, killer whales pose the greatest threat. Some orca populations have learned to hunt sea otters deliberately. This behavior has caused sharp population declines in parts of the Aleutian Islands. Unlike sharks, orcas actively target otters as prey.

Bald Eagles: Very young sea otter pups are vulnerable to bald eagles. Eagles may snatch pups floating at the surface while their mothers dive for food. These attacks are rare but almost always deadly for the pup.

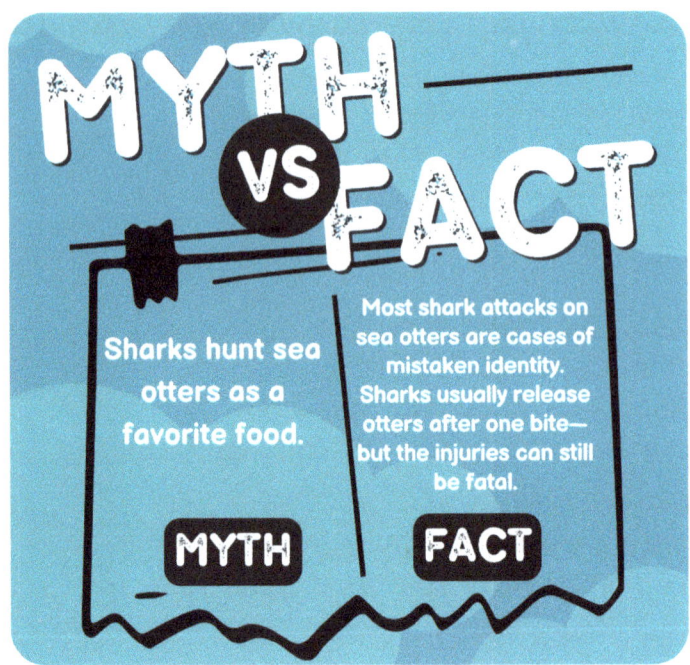

Steller Sea Lions: Steller sea lions are enormous—sometimes weighing over 1,000 pounds. In areas where their habitats overlap, they may attack sea otters during territorial disputes. These encounters are usually not for food, but the size difference makes them extremely dangerous.

Defense Strategies

Sea otters have evolved several ways to stay safe:
- **Safety in Numbers:** Otters rest in rafts, allowing many eyes to watch for danger
- **Alarm Calls:** Otters warn each other with sharp calls when predators appear
- **Quick Dives:** They can dive suddenly to escape birds and surface threats
- **Kelp Cover:** Dense kelp forests provide hiding places where large predators struggle to move
- **Agile Swimming:** Otters twist and turn underwater to evade attacks

Despite these defenses, predation is a natural part of ocean life. Predators help keep ecosystems balanced, and sea otters have evolved to survive alongside these dangers for thousands of years.

Challenges and Threats

Aside from natural predators, sea otters face many serious threats. From oil spills to warming oceans, their coastal world is changing rapidly, often in ways that put their survival at risk.

One of the greatest dangers is **oil pollution**. Sea otters rely entirely on their thick fur to stay warm, and even a small amount of oil can destroy its insulating ability. Oiled otters quickly become hypothermic, and without immediate rescue and cleaning, they often die.

Fishing activities create multiple threats. Otters get entangled in nets and traps. Depletion of fish stocks affects the broader ecosystem supporting otter prey. Competition with humans for shellfish limits food availability.

Climate change adds new challenges. Warming oceans, shifting prey populations, and stronger storms disrupt food availability and shelter. In some areas, sea otters struggle to find enough clams, crabs, and urchins to meet their daily needs.

Disease outbreaks are an increasing concern. A parasite called *Toxoplasma gondii*, often traced to cat waste washing into the ocean, can cause deadly brain infections in sea otters. Other diseases spread quickly in areas where otters gather in large groups.

Chemicals from land, like pesticides and herbicides, enter coastal waters through runoff. These pollutants build up in the marine food web, affecting sea otter health, reproduction, and immune systems. Plastic pollution also poses risks through entanglement or accidental ingestion.

Human disturbance disrupts normal behavior. Boat traffic, kayakers, and coastal development force otters to abandon prime habitat. Even well-meaning wildlife watchers can cause harm by getting too close.

Limited **genetic diversity** remains a concern, especially for California otters descended from a tiny group of survivors. This makes populations more vulnerable to disease and environmental changes.

Habitat loss continues as coastal development fragments nearshore ecosystems. Marina construction and coastal modifications eliminate critical habitat and disrupt kelp forests.

Despite these challenges, conservation efforts have helped many sea otter populations recover. Protecting their habitat, reducing pollution, and giving them space to thrive are key to ensuring their future.

How You Can Protect Sea Otter

- 🌍 Support marine protected areas
- 🍶 Reduce plastic use—it ends up in the ocean!
- 🐟 Choose sustainable seafood
- 🐱 Keep cats indoors (prevents Toxoplasma)
- 💡 Support clean energy to fight climate change
- 🛢 Report oil spills immediately
- 📓 Learn and share information about ocean conservation

Life Span and Population

Sea otters in the wild typically live 15 to 20 years, though some can reach 25 years or more. Females usually live longer than males, partly because males face greater risks from fights and predators. In human care, where food and medical treatment are provided, sea otters may live slightly longer.

The sea otter recovery story is one of conservation's greatest successes. In the early 1900s, hunting for their incredibly soft fur nearly wiped them out. The global population dropped to just 1,000–2,000 individuals, scattered across the North Pacific.

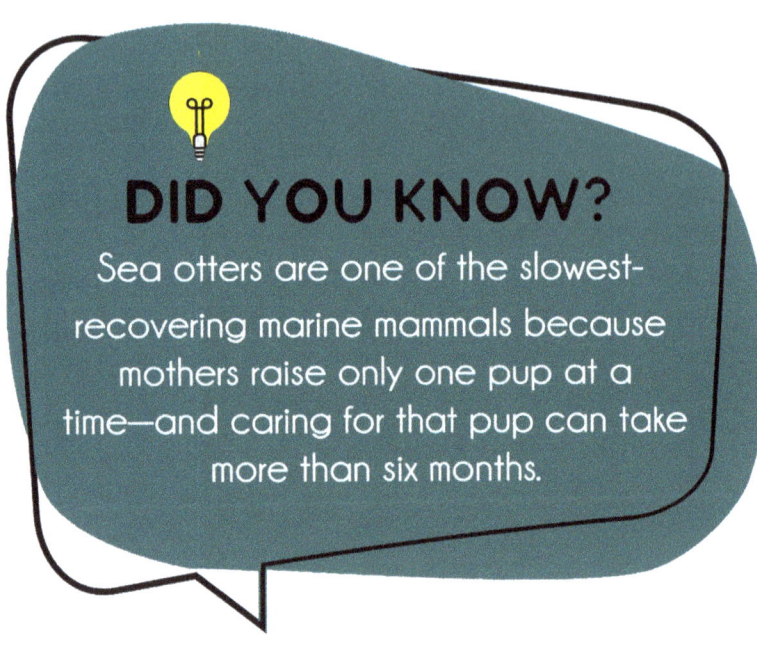

DID YOU KNOW? Sea otters are one of the slowest-recovering marine mammals because mothers raise only one pup at a time—and caring for that pup can take more than six months.

Today, an estimated 125,000–150,000 sea otters live in Pacific waters. While this is an impressive comeback, it is still below historical numbers that may have reached 150,000–300,000 before large-scale hunting began. Recovery has also been uneven, with some populations growing while others struggle.

Alaska is home to the vast majority of sea otters, with about 90,000–100,000 individuals. Large populations live in the Aleutian Islands, Prince William Sound, and Southeast Alaska. However, some Alaskan regions have experienced significant declines linked to increased killer whale predation and environmental changes.

California's southern sea otter population is much smaller, numbering around 3,000 individuals. Although this group has grown slowly in recent decades, it remains far below its historic range, which once extended from Baja California to Oregon.

Sea otters living along the coasts of Russia and nearby regions number roughly 15,000–20,000. These populations are relatively stable but face ongoing threats from oil development and fishing activity.

Several factors limit sea otter recovery. Females usually give birth to only one pup every one to two years, which slows population growth. Their high food needs and extreme sensitivity to pollution also make them vulnerable to environmental changes.

Scientists continue to closely monitor sea otter populations. Because otters play such an important role in coastal ecosystems, their numbers provide valuable clues about the overall health of the ocean.

Conclusion

Sea otters are far more than just cute faces in kelp forests. They're ecosystem engineers, tool users, devoted parents, and remarkable survivors whose presence transforms entire underwater worlds.

From their incredibly dense fur to their sophisticated tool use, sea otters demonstrate nature's amazing ability to adapt to challenging environments. Their playful behavior and social bonds remind us that intelligence and emotion aren't limited to land animals—the ocean is full of complex, feeling creatures deserving our respect and protection.

As keystone species, sea otters demonstrate how closely connected ecosystems truly are. When otters thrive, kelp forests flourish, fish populations grow, and coastal habitats remain balanced. When otters disappear, those systems begin to unravel.

Their recovery from near extinction proves conservation works when people commit to it! Laws protecting sea otters, habitat restoration, and public education have all contributed to this comeback story.

Yet challenges remain. Climate change, pollution, disease, and human disturbance continue threatening populations. Their slow reproduction and specific needs make them vulnerable to rapid environmental changes.

The future depends on our continued commitment to ocean conservation. By reducing pollution, protecting marine habitats, supporting sustainable fishing, and addressing climate change, we help ensure these remarkable animals survive and thrive.

Every time we see a sea otter floating peacefully, cracking open a sea urchin or holding hands with a companion, we're witnessing millions of years of evolution and life's resilience. These moments remind us the ocean isn't just water—it's a complex community of interdependent lives.

Sea otters have captured hearts worldwide, serving as ambassadors for marine conservation. Their story shows that with knowledge, dedication, and respect for nature, we can be partners in protecting the incredible diversity that makes our planet extraordinary.

Test Your Sea Otter Knowledge!

How much have you learned about sea otters? Try this quiz to find out!

1. What makes sea otter fur special?
    a) It changes color b) It's the densest fur of any animal c) It glows in the dark
    d) It never grows back

2. How long can a sea otter hold its breath underwater?
    a) 30 seconds b) 2 minutes c) Up to 5 minutes d) 10 minutes

3. What percentage of their body weight do sea otters eat daily?
    a) 5-10% b) 10-15% c) 20-25% d) 50%

4. What is a group of sea otters called?
    a) A pod b) A raft c) A herd d) A school

5. Why do sea otters hold hands while sleeping?
    a) To stay warm b) To prevent drifting apart c) To communicate d) To share food

6. What tool do sea otters use to crack open shellfish?
    a) Sticks b) Shells c) Rocks d) Coral

7. How many hairs per square inch can sea otters have?
    a) 1,000 b) 10,000 c) 100,000 d) Up to 1 million

8. What is sea otters' most important prey for the ecosystem?
    a) Fish b) Sea urchins c) Crabs d) Clams

9. How many sea otters were left in the early 1900s?
    a) 100-200 b) 1,000-2,000 c) 10,000-20,000 d) 50,000

10. What makes sea otters a "keystone species"?
    a) They're the biggest marine mammal   b) They eat the most food c) Their presence has huge impact on the ecosystem d) They're the smartest ocean animal

Answer Key: 1-b, 2-c, 3-c, 4-b, 5-b, 6-c, 7-d, 8-b, 9-b, 10-c

STEM Challenge: Think Like a Scientist!

Sea otters have amazing adaptations that help them survive in cold ocean waters. Try these fun, hands-on science experiments to discover how their bodies and behaviors help them thrive in the kelp forest!

Fur Insulation Test

Topic: Adaptation & Heat Transfer

You'll Need:
2 small bowls, 2 ice cubes, 2 resealable plastic bags, cotton balls (or wool, paper towels), timer.

What to Do:
1. Place one ice cube inside a plastic bag surrounded by cotton (this is your "sea otter fur").
2. Place another ice cube in a plain bag with no insulation.
3. Set both in bowls to catch drips.
4. Check every 5 minutes—which ice cube melts slower?

What You'll Learn:

Sea otter fur is the densest in the animal kingdom, with up to 1 million hairs per square inch that trap air, keeping warmth in and cold out—just like the cotton around your ice cube!

Rock Tool Engineering

Topic: Physics & Engineering

You'll Need:
Walnuts in shells, various rocks (flat and round), cardboard or wooden board, timer, safety goggles.

What to Do:
1. Try cracking walnuts using different shaped rocks.
2. Place a walnut on a flat rock (your "anvil") and hit it with another rock.
3. Try different rock combinations—which works best?
4. Time yourself cracking 5 walnuts—can you get faster with practice?

What You'll Learn:
Sea otters are one of the few marine mammals that use tools! They carry favorite rocks in skin pockets and use them as hammers and anvils—just like you did. Flat rocks make better anvils because they provide a stable surface.

 # Word Search

```
K F N I Y S E A U R C H I N S
I O O J N E S O O C E A N S X
G O I P R S A H V Z V S H V K
Q D T S R E P P I L F W J Q Y
E W A N E E U M A M M A L S S
P E V D D N D D K N P M B N K
O B R I W Z U A S C S I O L E
P M E Z N Q O P T T F I H R T
U E S C N S U C F O T J G S I
L T N T L P U A K A R N Z E U
A S O A V I R L T V I S V A R
T Y C T W J M P A M Q C M O C
I S G I K K A A O T D F N T K
O O J B Y D U O T H I E P T E
N C K A A F R R C E U O G E L
O E C H C G T K F O Y A N R P
P M Y S E R O V I N R A C L F
H O M E R A N G E P S A C R O
```

Adaptations Grooming Orcas
Carnivores Habitat Population
Climate Home Range Predators
Conservation Insulation Pups
Ecosystem Kelp Rafts
Flippers Mammals Sea Otter
Food Web Ocean Sea Urchins

Glossary

Adaptation: A special feature or behavior that helps an animal survive in its environment.

Carnivore: An animal that eats meat. Sea otters are carnivores that eat shellfish, crabs, sea urchins, and fish.

Conservation: Protecting animals, plants, and their habitats from harm or extinction.

Ecosystem: A community of living things and their environment working together.

Foraging: Searching for and gathering food.

Habitat: The natural home environment where an animal lives.

Keystone Species: An animal whose presence has a huge impact on its ecosystem.

Mammal: A warm-blooded animal that has fur and feeds milk to its babies.

Metabolism: The process by which the body converts food into energy.

Predator: An animal that hunts and eats other animals.

Prey: An animal that is hunted and eaten by predators.

Territory: An area that an animal defends as its own home range.

Trophic Cascade: When changes at one level of the food chain create effects throughout the ecosystem.

Urchin Barren: An underwater desert created when too many sea urchins eat all the kelp.

Vibrissae: The scientific name for whiskers.

Weaning: When a young mammal stops drinking its mother's milk and begins eating solid food.

Resources and References

Want to learn more about sea otters and ocean conservation? Check out these trusted books, websites, and organizations that explore wildlife, science, and conservation across the Pacific coast.

Books

Sea Otter Heroes: The Predators That Saved an Ecosystem by Patricia Newman (Millbrook Press) — Discover how sea otters transformed California's kelp forests.

Sea Otters by Melissa Gish (Creative Education) — Beautiful photos and detailed facts about these marine mammals.

A Place for Sea Otters by Melissa Stewart (Peachtree Publishing) — Learn how sea otters shape their ocean homes.

Websites

Monterey Bay Aquarium – Sea Otters
montereybayaquarium.org/animals/sea-otter
Watch live sea otter cams and learn about their care and conservation.

National Geographic Kids – Sea Otter Facts
kids.nationalgeographic.com/animals/mammals/facts/sea-otter
Explore sea otter behavior, habitat, and amazing adaptations.

Sea Otter Savvy
seaottersavvy.org
Learn how to watch sea otters responsibly and protect their habitats.

U.S. Fish and Wildlife Service – Southern Sea Otter
fws.gov/species/southern-sea-otter
Track recovery efforts and learn about sea otter conservation programs.

For Young Scientists

NOAA Ocean Exploration – Kelp Forests
oceanexploration.noaa.gov
Explore kelp forest ecosystems and the animals that depend on them.

Monterey Bay National Marine Sanctuary
montereybay.noaa.gov
Discover the protected waters where California sea otters live and thrive.

Keep Exploring!

If you enjoyed learning about sea otters, explore other titles in the This Incredible Planet series to discover more amazing animals—from sea turtles to penguins to elephants—and the habitats they call home.

Index

A
adaptations, 12
Alaska, 11, 32
appearance, 8

B
bald eagles, 28
birth, 23
breeding, 23

C
California, 11, 16, 28, 32
Canada, 11
carnivores, 15
challenges, 31
chemicals, 31
climate change, 31
communication, 16
conservation, 7, 31
courtship, 23

D
daily activity, 20
defense strategies, 28
diet, 15, 20
disease, 31

E
ecosystems, 7, 27
environment, 7, 11

F
females, 8, 16, 23, 32
fishing, 31
food, 15, 20
food webs, 27
fur, 8, 12, 20, 24

G
genetic diversity, 31
great white sharks, 28
grooming, 20

H
habitat, 7, 11
habitat loss, 31
human disruption, 31

K
kelp forests, 7, 11, 27
keystone species, 27
killer whales, 28

L
life span, 32

M
males, 8, 16, 19, 23
marine mammals, 7
mating, 23
migration, 18–19

O
oil pollution, 31
orcas, 28

P
parenting, 23, 24
pesticides, 31
physical adaptations, 12
physical appearance, 8
pollution, 31
population, 32
predators, 28
pregnancy, 23
pups, 23, 24

R
rafts, 16, 20
reproduction, 23
river otters, 7
Russia, 32

S
sea lions, 28
sea urchins, 15, 26, 27
seals, 7
seasons, 19
sharks, 28
size, 8
sleep, 20
social behavior, 16
speed, 19
stellar sea lions, 28

T
tails, 8
territories, 11
threats, 31
tool use, 7, 8, 12, 15
Toxoplasma gondii, 31

W
weasels, 7
whiskers, 12

www.ingramcontent.com/pod-product-compliance
Lightning Source LLC
Chambersburg PA
CBHW040224040426
42333CB00051B/3439